Cr

D0992215

512

SITTING BULL

Lakota Leader
by Catherine Iannone

A Book Report Biography
FRANKLIN WATTS
A Division of Grolier Publishing
New York / London / Hong Kong / Sydney
Danbury, Connecticut

Photographs ©: American Heritage Center, University of Wyoming: 26, 55; Archive Photos: 32, 82; Denver Public Library, Western History Department: 61; Detroit Public Library: 76; Minnesota Historical Society: 43; Montana Historical Society: 72; North Wind Picture Archives: 10, 13; Smithsonian Institution: 17, 97; Superstock, Inc.: 48 (Private Collection/ A.K.G., Berlin/SuperStock), 2, 69, 89; Texas State Archives: 20; U.S. Signal Corps: 36; UPI/Corbis-Bettmann: 41, 59, 74, 88, 91.

Visit Franklin Watts on the Internet at:
http://publishing.grolier.com

Library of Congress Cataloging-in-Publication Data

Iannone, Catherine.
Sitting Bull: lakota leader / by Catherine Iannone.
    p. cm.- (A book report biography)
Includes bibliographical references and index.
Summary: Discusses the life of the Hunkpapa chief who is remembered for his defeat of General Custer at Little Bighorn and provides a history of the Lakota Indians who were his people.
    ISBN 0-531-11426-0 (lib. bdg.)   0-531-15934-5 (pbk.)
    1. Sitting Bull, 1834?-1890—Juvenile literature. 2. Hunkpapa Indians—Biography—Juvenile literature. 3. Dakota Indians—Biography—Juvenile literature. [1. Sitting Bull,1834?-1890. 2. Hunkpapa Indians—Biography. 3. Indians of North America—Great Plains—Biography. 4. Dakota Indians—History.] I. Series.
E99.D1S6054   1998
978'.004975'0092—dc21
[B]   97-32391
                                                              CIP
                                                               AC

CONTENTS

Lakota chief, warrior, and medicine man, Sitting Bull has become one of the great legends of the American West. This thrilling biography takes you along with Sitting Bull as he fights General Custer and his men at the Battle of Little Bighorn, flees to Canada, becomes a star in Buffalo Bill's Wild West Show, and tragically dies on a reservation in North Dakota.

CHAPTER 1

COUNTING COUP

Hunkesni watched closely as his father and the other members of the war party prepared to meet the enemy. The horses were fed and painted red for battle. The men discussed their plans while crafting new arrows and repairing their bows. The women sewed moccasins for the journey and prepared pemmican, a combination of dried buffalo meat and berries that would keep during a long trip.

Hunkesni's father and uncle, Four Horns and Looks-for-Him-in-a-Tent, were chiefs who were known for their bravery in battle. And among the Lakota Indians, warfare was the testing ground of all men. Through warfare, the Lakota Indians had acquired vast hunting grounds. They captured horses that allowed them to follow the herds of buffalo on which they depended for survival. In Lakota society, a boy could prove himself to be a man only by demonstrating the skills and bravery of a warrior.

*American Indians learned to ride on the
side of a horse to protect themselves
from enemy arrows and bullets.*

Hunkesni felt great admiration for the men
who were going to war. All his life he had listened
to the warriors tell stories about their brave
deeds. He had often seen war parties return to the
village, singing songs of victory. During the feast
that followed their return, the warriors would
recount their victories and be rewarded with honors. Like all Lakota boys, Hunkesni had spent
most of his time playing games that honed his
skills as a warrior. He had already become a mas-
terful horseman and had practiced dodging bul-

lets and arrows by leaning over the side of his horse, using the animal's body as a shield. And he had proven his shooting skill when he killed his first buffalo at the age of ten. Now, at fourteen, Hunkesni was ready to prove himself as a warrior.

As the warriors assembled, Hunkesni rode up on his gray horse and declared that he would join them. His father was proud of the boy's courage and did not try to stop him. Going on a *raid* would be a good experience, even though he was too young to fight. He told his son to be brave and handed him a *coup stick*.

Hunkesni was thrilled at the thought of using this weapon, for the coup stick was used in the most dangerous, and therefore the most admired, kind of fighting. Unlike arrows, which could be shot from a distance, a coup stick could be used only when fighting very close to an enemy. Hitting an enemy with a coup stick, known as "counting coup," was the bravest accomplishment in battle. Up to four warriors could count coup on a single enemy, but the highest honors went to the man who reached the enemy first and counted first coup on him.

Hunkesni rode proudly beside his father. For three days, the war party rode in search of their enemy, the Crow, hoping to return home with horses as well as Crow scalps and tales of bravery that would gain the respect of the tribe. Finally, a group of Crow were spotted. Hunkesni

The counting coup is awarded to the warrior who kills an enemy. Sitting Bull, who hit the enemy first, received the honor of first coup.

was ready for battle, dressed only in moccasins, a breechcloth tied around his waist, and beads hung around his neck. His entire body was painted yellow.

As the Lakotas charged toward the enemy, one of the Crow tried to flee. Hunkesni shouted a war cry and took off after the lone Crow. As his horse caught up, Hunkesni lifted his coup stick and hit the Crow, knocking him off his horse. Another Lakota rode up and killed the man, but the glory of counting first coup belonged to Hunkesni. At the age of fourteen, he had proven himself to be a man. He was now a warrior.

When the war party returned to the village, word of Hunkesni's bravery spread like wildfire. His father held a feast in the boy's honor and told everyone of his accomplishment. Hunkesni's body was painted black as a sign of victory, and a white eagle feather was placed in his hair to commemorate his first coup. His father gave him a weapon to use in the many battles that would follow—a lance, 7 feet long (2 meters) with a sharp iron blade. His mother, Her-Holy-Door, had decorated the handle of the lance with blue and white beads. He was also given a shield made of rawhide and covered with soft buckskin, on which a holy man had painted a design that Hunkesni's father had seen in a dream, thus endowing the shield with sacred power. This shield would protect him in battle throughout his life.

Finally his father gave him an even greater honor. He gave Hunkesni his own name. *Hunkesni*, which means "slow," was a nickname that the boy had gained as an infant. From now on, the boy who had been known as Slow would take his father's name, *Tatanka-Iyotanka*, or Sitting Bull. And from this point on, his father would be known as Jumping Bull.

According to Sitting Bull biographer Robert M. Utley, "The name Sitting Bull, according to fellow tribesmen, suggested an animal possessed of great endurance, his build much admired by the people, and when brought to bay planted immovably on his haunches to fight on to the death." Sitting Bull would soon prove deserving of this favorable name, and in the coming years his bravery would be known throughout Lakota territory. The name Sitting Bull would inspire the fear and respect not only of the neighboring Crow and Assiniboine tribes but also of the *wasichus*, the word used by the Lakota for the white citizens of the ever-expanding United States.

> **"The name Sitting Bull, according to fellow tribesmen, suggested an animal possessed of great endurance."**

CHAPTER 2

HUNKPAPA

At the time of Sitting Bull's birth, sometime in the early 1830s, the Lakota had little to fear from the wasichus. Although the wasichus had conquered many tribes and seized their lands, the settlers had little interest in the *Great Plains*, where the Lakota made their home. Being used to the wooded and mountainous landscape of Europe and the twenty-four states, they found the Great Plains, with their endless expanses of flat, treeless landscape and scarcity of water, uninviting. During the summer, the sun beat down mercilessly, scorching the prairie grass, which covered the land as far as the eye could see. In winter, temperatures plunged well below zero and massive blizzards buried the region under mounds of snow.

In this foreign environment, the settlers were unable to build houses and fuel their fires without timber. Because the Great Plains were thought to

The Lakota used buffalo skin to construct their teepees. In this photograph, Lakota women stretch buffalo skins out to dry in the sun.

be useless to white settlers, they were left to the American Indians, and the U.S. Army built forts just east of the plains to mark the boundary known as the Permanent Indian Frontier. For a time, the Lakotas' territory was free from the white invaders. Although the Lakota had virtually no contact with whites, their way of life was dramatically affected by the arrival of Europeans in North America.

The Lakota were buffalo hunters who rode over the Great Plains on horseback and lived in tepees, but this lifestyle had existed for only about a century before Sitting Bull's birth. Until that time, the Lakota had lived in the woods of Minnesota in wigwams—huts made of a framework of arched poles covered with bark. They sustained themselves by gathering wild rice, hunting deer and smaller game, and fishing in the many streams and lakes that dotted the woodland. They traveled on foot and used dogs to carry their supplies on a travois, an A-shaped frame made of two poles connected by a platform; the poles were fastened to the shoulders of a dog and dragged on the ground.

As European settlers arrived on the eastern coast of the present-day United States, the tribes who lived there were either wiped out or forced westward. Eventually, the Lakota's homeland in Minnesota was invaded by the Cree and Ojibwa tribes. They overpowered the Lakota with the guns they had received from French fur traders in Canada. The Lakota were pushed westward onto the wide-open prairies of the Great Plains. There they found enormous herds of buffalo that could supply not only abundant meat but most of the other necessities of life as well. Without tree bark to make their houses, the Lakota began building tepees made of buffalo hides.

Another Sioux group, the Dakota or Santee, remained in Minnesota and continued to lead the kind of life the Lakota had known. The Yankton and Yanktonai Sioux lived east of the Missouri River, in the area between the Lakota and the Dakota territories. They took up buffalo hunting but held on to more of their old ways than did the Lakota.

Both *Dakota* and *Lakota* mean "ally." When the French first encountered the Dakota, they used the name that the Ojibwa called them— *natowessiw*, which means "enemies." The French shortened the word to *Sioux*.

Before the Lakota could make a new home on the Plains, they had to win territory from the tribes who were already living there. The Lakota became great warriors as they engaged in battle with the Crow, Kiowa, Pawnee, Omaha, and other tribes and pushed them from their home-lands.

The horse allowed the Lakota to follow and hunt down the buffalo.

The Lakota first rode horses in the middle of the eighteenth century. Horses had been introduced to the Americas by the Spanish, and horses that escaped from Spanish ranches in Mexico formed wild herds that roamed the Plains. The Lakota traded for horses with the tribes of the southern Plains, captured wild horses that wandered north into their territory, and stole horses from enemy tribes.

Soon the Lakota became expert riders, and the horse drastically changed their lifestyle. They could now travel quickly across the Plains in search of buffalo; and hunting on horseback enabled them to ride alongside the herds as they fired at the animals. Horses also made it easier to move camp, as horses could carry much more than dogs could. Around this time, the Lakota began to acquire guns through trade with French fur traders in Canada and raids on enemies.

The Lakota had an incredible ability to adapt to new circumstances. They soon became the most prosperous and powerful tribe on the Plains. By the early 1800s, the Lakota controlled a vast territory stretching from the Missouri River to the Bighorn Mountains, encompassing much of present-day North and South Dakota, Nebraska, Wyoming, and Montana.

The Lakota were made up of seven tribes. Sitting Bull belonged to the Hunkpapas, one of the smaller divisions. They lived in southwestern North Dakota and southeastern Montana. The other divisions were the Oglalas, Brules, Miniconjous, Two Kettles, Sans Arcs, and the Blackfeet.

The young Sitting Bull was proud of his heritage and strove to attain the virtues that made a Lakota man great. He had already proven his bravery on the battlefield, but it took more than war honors to win the respect of his people. The most admired trait among the Lakota was generosity. People were respected not for possessing wealth but for giving food, horses, and other prized possessions to those in need. Sitting Bull displayed this virtue at a young age. When he killed his first buffalo at the age of ten, he gave the meat to a family that had no horses and so could not easily hunt.

Even as a youth, the strength of his character was apparent. According to one account, when Sitting Bull was seventeen years old, a war party returned to his camp with a Crow woman they had taken captive. They intended to adopt her into the tribe, as the Lakota often did with women and children who were captured in *raids*. However, the women spoke to the captive and determined that she was an immoral woman. The Lakota placed a high value upon women's chastity, and they wanted to punish this woman.

The Lakota women tore off the captive's clothes and prepared to burn her at the stake. As they tied her up and gathered dry brush around her feet, Sitting Bull heard the screams of the helpless captive and wanted to end her suffering. He was too young to stop the execution. However, before the fire could be lit at her feet, Sitting Bull drew his bow and shot an arrow through the woman's heart, killing her instantly and sparing her the torture of being burned alive.

This story demonstrates the power of Sitting Bull's convictions. He was not afraid of incurring the anger of his people in order to uphold his principles. And he also displayed a strong sense of mercy. Sitting Bull's peacelike qualities—generosity, mercy, kindness, and wisdom—along with his skills as a hunter and warrior made him a model of Lakota manhood.

As a young warrior, Sitting Bull won many honors in battle with the Crow and Assiniboine. As he matured, he became an imposing presence on the battlefield with his broad, muscular frame, large head, and height of nearly six feet. He appeared even more fearsome in the regalia of the Strong Heart Society, the most prestigious warrior group of the Hunkpapa. He earned the honor of being one of two sash-wearers of the Strong Hearts.

The sash-wearers wore a headpiece covered with crow feathers and decorated with a buffalo horn above each ear as well as a sash that hung from one shoulder and reached the ground. These warriors were called upon to demonstrate their bravery in battle by driving a lance into the ground through the end of the sash so that they were fixed to one spot. They had to hold their ground until they achieved victory or were released by a fellow warrior.

Sitting Bull, through his numerous victories and feats of bravery, became so feared by his enemies that warriors would intimidate the enemy by shouting, "Tatanka-Iyotanka he miye" (Sitting Bull, I am he!) or "Tatanka-Iyotanka tahoksila" (We are Sitting Bull's boys!).

While Sitting Bull was emerging as a leader, a new sense of tribal unity was growing among the Hunkpapa and the other Lakota tribes. The Lakota had traditionally lived in *bands*—groups of households linked by ties of kinship. Each band had its own leaders and made its own decisions about hunting and warfare and relocating camp. Sometimes several bands joined together for hunts, and occasionally the entire tribe came together. At these times, a council of the more experienced and esteemed men would meet to discuss matters that concerned all the bands, but there were no leaders who ruled the tribe as a whole. In 1851, however, the Hunkpapa named four "shirt-wearers," who would carry out the decisions of the council of tribal elders. One of these shirt-wearers was Sitting Bull's uncle Four Horns.

Perhaps this surge of tribal unity was brought on by the presence of a new enemy. In 1851, the tribes of the Plains had their first contact with representatives of the United States government. Previously, the only whites in the vicinity were the traders at Fort Pierre, on the Missouri River. The fort, which was known to the Sioux as Wornout Fences, had been built shortly after Sitting Bull's birth. Lakota bands, including Sitting Bull's, would occasionally visit the fort to trade buffalo hides for guns and ammunition, as well as for other goods valued by the Lakota, including metal tools, pots, and glass beads. But the Lakota had never dealt with a government agent or encountered the U.S. Army.

Now, however, the United States had an interest in the Great Plains, but only as a *way station*. Settlers were now heading for the Pacific coast, some following the lure of the California gold rush that had begun two years earlier. Others were seeking the fertile lands of Oregon, which had recently become a U.S. territory after a long dispute with England. These settlers followed the Oregon Trail, which ran through the Great Plains south of Hunkpapa territory. Plains tribes that had encountered wagon trains carrying settlers westward did not appreciate their presence and sometimes attacked. Some of these travelers also became caught between two warring tribes. If the United States was going to expand to the Pacific, the government would have to protect the settlers who tried to make their way there.

In September 1851, government agents invited the tribes of the northern plains to meet at Fort Laramie in Nevada Territory. Representatives of the Sioux, Cheyenne, Arapaho, Shoshone, Crow,

In 1851, tribal chiefs and government representatives met at Fort Laramie to discuss a new treaty.

Assiniboine, Arikara, Mandan, and Hidatsa gathered to hear the government's proposal for the Fort Laramie Treaty of 1851. According to this treaty, the U.S. government would build roads and forts on the Plains, and the Indians would stop attacking white settlers and other tribes. In order to end intertribal warfare, the permanent boundaries of each tribe's territory would be set. In return for the tribes' compliance with the treaty, the government promised to protect them from the white settlers and to pay $50,000 a year for fifteen years, to be divided among all the tribes that signed.

Although many Indians signed the treaty, there is no way they could have stuck to it. A major problem with such treaties was the lack of central authority in most tribes. Among the Lakota, for example, chiefs did not have the power to force all members of the tribe to obey an agreement. Going to battle was usually a personal decision for each warrior to make. In a society in which warfare was the main means for men to gain personal glory, it was impossible to stop men from going to war, especially young warriors like Sitting Bull, who still had a lot to prove.

Another flaw in the treaty was the absence of many tribes from the signing. The U.S. agents considered all Sioux to be a single tribe and did not summon representatives from the Dakota, Yankton, and Lakota. There was no representative of the Hunkpapa present at the treaty council, and in later years they would often be told that they were breaking the terms of a treaty they did not sign.

This confusing first encounter with whites would lead to endless troubles for the Lakota and their neighboring tribes. Soldiers streamed into the Plains to hold the Indians to a treaty that many of them neither wanted nor understood. It also marked the first of many instances in which the Indians would be torn between making concessions to the whites in exchange for peace or independence. This would cause major conflicts in every tribe.

The treaty's faults became obvious soon after it was signed. As more and more settlers crossed the Plains and army posts were built, the Indians became increasingly anxious. And the soldiers who were sent to protect the Indians from the white settlers, as agreed in the treaty, knew nothing about dealing with Indians.

The first serious repercussion of the Fort Laramie Treaty resulted from an ox that strayed from a wagon train on August 18, 1854. A Miniconjou named High Forehead came across the ox and killed it. The Mormon settlers reported the incident to the soldiers at Fort Laramie. The next day, a hotheaded young lieutenant named John L. Grattan led a force of thirty men to the Brule village of Conquering Bear, where High Forehead was visiting. As they set out, Grattan told his men, "I do not expect to be compelled to fire a single gun, but I hope to God we will have a fight."

It is no surprise then that the arrest of a single Lakota turned into a bloodbath. But the fight did not fulfill Grattan's hopes. After his men fired, mortally wounding Conquering Bear, the Brule fought back and soon killed Grattan and all his men.

News of this incident, known as the Grattan Massacre, spread quickly and caused outrage in Washington, where news of the "massacre" failed to mention that it had been started by the U.S. Army. Reinforcements were sent to the area to punish the Lakota and to prevent them from causing more trouble. The Brule village in which the massacre had occurred was destroyed, and all men, women, and children were killed or taken captive.

As the Lakota witnessed such horrors and the army became a more prominent presence in their region, it was clear that the wasichus were a dire threat. And as Sitting Bull grew into a leader, he learned the facts that would forever influence his relations with the U.S. government and its citizens: the wasichus could not be trusted, and entering into agreements with them was a dangerous proposition.

CHAPTER 3

A WARRIOR'S LIFE

During these tumultuous times, Sitting Bull was among those who refused to give up the life and privileges of a warrior. He continued to gain honors, and at the age of twenty-five he became famous for his exploits during a raiding expedition for Crow horses.

A small group of warriors snuck into a Crow village in the night while Sitting Bull and the rest of the raiding party waited outside the village, ready to speed home with the newly won horses. As the Crow slept, a large herd was driven from the camp. A few Lakotas led the horses home while most of the warriors rode behind the herd, ready for an attack. Sunrise was approaching. The Crow would soon awake and discover the theft, and they still had enough horses to carry a large contingent of warriors in pursuit of the raiders.

With the first light of day, the Lakota heard the enraged Crow approaching. As the two sides clashed, the Lakota overpowered their enemies and the Crow began to retreat. The raiding party prepared to ride home in victory when suddenly a lone Crow charged at them. Sitting Bull accepted the challenge and ran toward the warrior, who wore the red shirt that marked him as a Crow chief. As the two approached each other on foot, both armed with a musket, the chief recognized the Strong Heart bonnet and sash and knew that he faced a worthy opponent.

The two warriors fired almost simultaneously. Sitting Bull hit his mark, killing the chief. The chief's bullet flew through the shield that Jumping Bull had given his son and tore through Sitting Bull's foot. Sitting Bull stood in spite of the gash that ran through the length of his foot, demonstrating the strength that was cultivated in Lakota warriors. He walked to the chief's body, cut off the scalp, and rode home. His foot was treated when he reached camp, but the wound left him with a limp that would last the rest of his life. In spite of his injury, Sitting Bull remained a powerful warrior, and in 1857 he was named a war chief of the Hunkpapa.

Sitting Bull's fearsome reputation on the battlefield was balanced by his kindness to his own people and his efforts to keep the peace among

By the time he was a young man, Sitting Bull had won the respect and admiration of his tribe.

them. One member of Sitting Bull's camp said, "There was something in Sitting Bull that everybody liked. Children liked him because he was good, the women because he was kind to the family and liked to settle family troubles. Men liked him because he was brave. Medicine men liked him because they knew he was a man they could consider a leader."

> **"There was something in Sitting Bull that everybody liked."**

Sitting Bull won the respect of the medicine men because of his status as a Wichasa Wakan, or holy man. Sitting Bull had a close connection with *Wakantanka*, the sacred power that is present throughout the universe. Sitting Bull always strove to learn about this power, which, according to Sioux beliefs, existed in everything. Every tree, stone, and animal, as well as the air and the clouds and the earth contained this great spirit. The buffalo, which provided the Lakota with most of their needs, were believed to be especially sacred. The Lakota had great respect for them, and after a hunt they offered a prayer of thanks to the animals for giving the gift of their bodies so that the people could live.

Sitting Bull spent much of his youth observing nature and trying to understand its mysteries.

He learned a great deal from his family, especially his father, Jumping Bull; his mother, Her-Holy-Door; and his uncle, Four Horns. Like his father, Sitting Bull possessed both the gift of prophecy and the ability to communicate with animals. In fact, according to legend, the names Sitting Bull and Jumping Bull had been given to Sitting Bull's father by a buffalo. And Sitting Bull used to tell a story about a bird that saved his life.

While on a hunting trip, Sitting Bull stopped to rest beneath some trees near the bank of the Grand River. As he fell asleep, he saw a woodpecker looking at him from a nearby tree. He was soon startled from his sleep by the sound of a grizzly bear coming at him. He was terrified, knowing that his arrows would be no match for the enormous beast. Suddenly he heard the woodpecker knock on the tree and say, "Lie still! Lie still!" Sitting Bull followed the bird's advice as the bear approached. The bear continued on its way, taking no interest in the motionless body. When Sitting Bull opened his eyes, the bird was still watching him. Sitting Bull had a talent for composing songs, and he sang to the bird, "Pretty bird, you saw me and took pity on me; You wish me to survive among the people. O Bird People, from this day always you shall be my relatives!"

For all Wichasa Wakan, a pivotal point in their spiritual life was the *vision quest* they experienced between the ages of ten and fourteen. The vision quest was a very personal experience during which a boy would be visited by a spirit, often in the form of an animal. This spirit would guide and protect the boy for the rest of his life. A boy who sought a vision received advice from a holy man, although the vision quest was done in solitude.

The boy went to an isolated hilltop where he fasted and prayed for a vision. Afterward, he would speak of the vision to the holy man, who interpreted it and helped the boy create sacred objects that could be used to summon the powers of the spirit. Because this was such a personal experience, we have no way of knowing what Sitting Bull saw in his vision, but he was known among his people as being surrounded by sacred power.

The Lakota often came in contact with the spiritual world through their dreams. Men who had similar dreams would join together in dream societies that held ceremonies to pay homage to the spirits they had seen. Sitting Bull belonged to at least two of these societies the Buffalo Society and the Thunder Bird Society. It was believed that only the most blessed men dreamed of the thunderbird.

Sitting Bull also demonstrated his spiritual development by participating in the festival of the

A Lakota Sun Dance

Sun Dance. Each June, the tribe gathered for this twelve-day festival, during which women and men carried out sacred rituals. The festival culminated in the Sun Dance, a ceremony in which men endured varying degrees of self-sacrifice to Wakantanka. Some danced while looking at the sun until they fell exhausted. Others made a sacrifice of their flesh. First, they drove wooden skewers through the muscles on several parts of the body. These were attached to ropes that were tied to a tall pole, around which the men danced, pulling against the rope. They did not stop dancing until the skewers ripped through their flesh. The sacrifice of one's own body in this way was seen as the greatest sign of devotion, and Sitting Bull was said to have borne the scars of many Sun Dances.

Sitting Bull's strong attachment to Wakantanka and the spirits of the natural world were believed to be the basis of his strength on the battlefield. However, he rarely prayed for himself. His prayers and offerings were always made in order to benefit the entire tribe.

Added to Sitting Bull's concern for his band and the tribe as a whole were his growing family responsibilities. The year of the Fort Laramie Treaty, he had married a woman named Light Hair. Sadly, the marriage was short-lived. Light Hair died while giving birth to their first child, a son. Their son lived only four years before falling to disease.

To compensate for this devastating loss, Sitting Bull adopted his nephew One Bull, the son of his sister Good Feather and the Miniconjou chief Makes Room. One Bull was the same age as Sitting Bull's son, and he remained with his uncle for most of Sitting Bull's life. One Bull's brother, White Bull, who was a few years older, remained with his parents. But he often visited his brother and uncle, and he would later accompany them to war. Both boys felt a deep love and respect for their uncle, and they learned a great deal from him. They excelled at warfare and hunting and won admiration for their intelligence and principles.

Sitting Bull's family grew again after a raid in Assiniboine territory, north of the Missouri River. The fight was bloody, and both sides lost men before the Assiniboine fled. One, however, was unable to escape—a boy about thirteen years old. As the Lakota tried to capture him, the boy drew an arrow and attempted to shoot, but the arrow slipped and the Hunkpapa descended upon him, ready to kill him. In desperation, the boy threw his arms around Sitting Bull and called him "older brother." Sitting Bull took pity on the young captive and, despite the opposition of the other warriors, decided to adopt him as a brother. The boy came to be known by several names, including Stays Back and Kills Plenty. He was given the permanent name Jumping Bull in 1859, after Sitting Bull's father was killed in a battle with the Crow.

As was normal in Sioux society, Sitting Bull brought two wives into the household, Snow-On-Her and Red Woman. The two women were jealous of each other, and the home was often filled with hostility.

After the death of Sitting Bull's father, his mother, Her-Holy-Door, moved into his household.

She had always been a strong influence in his life, and she would continue to advise him until her death twenty-six years later.

In the coming years, Sitting Bull would increasingly seek her advice as he took on more responsibility for the welfare of his people and as the white world closed in on them.

CHAPTER 4

THE WASICHUS

Two events that occurred beyond the boundaries of their territory in 1862 had grave consequences for the Lakota. First, gold was discovered in the Rocky Mountains. This meant a new influx of whites passing through the Lakota's land on their way west. The Indians had already been angered by the stream of wagon trains passing through their land; but now they grew furious, and their attacks on travelers increased.

The second incident took place among the Dakota, who still lived in the Lakota's former homeland in Minnesota. Like the Lakota, the Dakota had treaties forced upon them. But their land was wanted not only as a route west but also as a place for whites to live. In the preceding ten years, 150,000 whites had come to build homes in their territory. The Dakotas were left with only one-tenth of their land. The sudden growth in

The Plains Indians grew angry as the number
of settlers crossing their territory increased.

population had led to a decrease in the game they
depended on, and the Dakota were not able to
provide for themselves on such a small area of
land. Instead, they were expected to live on *annu-*
ities—food and supplies provided by the U.S. government.

In 1862, however, the annuities did not
arrive and the Dakota were facing starvation.
This situation, combined with the Dakota's anger
over the way the white settlers treated them, led
to an explosive situation. On August 17, four
young men attacked settlers near the town of

Acton, Minnesota, killing three men and two women. Soon others joined in the attacks and the U.S. Army was called in. After a month of bloody conflict, the Dakota were overpowered. Many of the warriors who had been most active during the fighting fled north to Canada or west in hope of finding refuge among the Lakota. Many who had not taken part in the fighting surrendered.

During the battle, Alexander Ramsey, the governor of Minnesota, had declared, "The Sioux Indians must be exterminated or driven forever beyond the borders of the state." Now he had the opportunity to make good on this threat. The

"The Sioux Indians must be exterminated"

Dakota were put on trial, and 303 Indians were sentenced to death. President Lincoln reviewed the records of the trials and most of the condemned were spared execution, but thirty-eight men were hanged. The next year, the remaining Dakota were sent to a *reservation* near the Missouri River in Lakota territory. Now all of the Dakota homeland was in the hands of white settlers.

In the summer of 1863, 5,000 U.S. troops under the command of General Henry H. Sibley swarmed into Lakota territory to hunt down the Dakotas who had fled during the war in Minnesota

*Minnesota Governor Alexander Ramsey was
determined to drive the Indians from the state.*

and to stop the Lakota from harassing white travelers. In July, Dakotas who were retreating from
a fight with Sibley fled to nearby Hunkpapa and
Blackfeet camps. When the troops came after the
Dakota, the Hunkpapa and Blackfeet joined in
the fight. After several battles that drove the

Indians farther west, General Sibley and his troops returned to Minnesota, leaving General Alfred Sully in command at Fort Pierre.

General Sully wasted no time in demonstrating the strength of his forces. On September 3, at the Battle of Whitestone Hill, U.S. soldiers killed 100 Indians, captured 156, and destroyed much of the food and possessions the Indians needed to survive the coming winter.

The winter was relatively peaceful, but when warm weather returned, so did the fighting. It came to a climax in July, as General Sully and 3,000 soldiers escorted a wagon train full of miners along the Cannonball River. The Sioux had joined forces, and thousands of Lakota, Yanktonai, and Dakota set up camp along the soldiers' route.

On July 28, the approaching soldiers were spotted. Sitting Bull and the other warriors prepared for battle. White Bull joined the warriors to fight his first battle, at the age of fourteen, as his uncle had done. They were confident that the soldiers would be no match for such a large group of Sioux warriors, so they did not take the precaution of moving the camp, with the women, children, and old people, a safe distance from the battle.

But the army's rifles and cannon overpowered the Sioux arrows and muskets. The Battle of Killdeer Mountain ended with more than 100

Indians killed. Four Horns was shot in the back, but Sitting Bull treated the wound and his uncle recovered. As the soldiers defeated the Sioux warriors, they moved toward the camp. The Sioux fled to the safety of the Little Missouri Badlands, where the rough terrain prevented the soldiers from pursuing them. They had to leave behind almost all of their belongings, and the next day, the soldiers burned everything. The Sioux were left without food and shelter.

In August, a three-day battle ended with the Sioux once again retreating. Later that month, while looking for buffalo, Sitting Bull and a few Hunkpapa bands saw fifty soldiers escorting another group of miners. On September 2, the Hunkpapa ambushed the wagon train. This time the advantage of surprise gave the Hunkpapa an edge over their opponents, but Sitting Bull was hit by a bullet in his hip. The battle ended with the Hunkpapa's attempt to obtain food in exchange for Fanny Kelly, a white woman who had been captured by the Oglala from a wagon train in July. The Oglala had traded Fanny Kelly to a Hunkpapa named Brings-Plenty, and he brought her into his household as a wife. The negotiations for her release failed and the Hunkpapa resumed their hunt.

Throughout this period, the U.S. Army became more of a presence among the Lakota.

Forts were springing up throughout their territory and more and more soldiers came to defend them. Many of the Lakota knew from the experience of the Dakota in Minnesota that fighting the U.S. Army would end with their lands being *confiscated.* They thought making peace with the whites was the only way to save themselves. Others learned from the Dakota's experience that making peace with the whites meant broken promises, an end to their way of life, and hunger. The rifts among the Lakota continued to grow.

On October 23, two hundred Hunkpapa and Blackfeet went to Fort Sully, where Bear's Rib, the representative of the peace-seeking Lakota, met with Captain John H. Pell. Captain Pell said the army would continue to wage war as long as the Lakota made trouble for white settlers. And he demanded that the Hunkpapa return Fanny Kelly immediately.

Sitting Bull did not want to go to war for the sake of a captive, but Brings-Plenty did not want to give up his wife. Sitting Bull intervened, saying to Brings-Plenty and the other Hunkpapa who did not wish to release her, "Friends, this woman is out of our path. Her path is different. You can see in her face that she is homesick and unhappy here. So I am going to send her back." Brings-Plenty finally agreed to let her go, and she was brought to Fort Sully.

The return of Fanny Kelly did not go far in easing tensions between the Lakota and the whites. News reached Lakota territory that convinced many that the whites had to be driven out. In November 1864, the Colorado militia had attacked a camp of friendly southern Cheyennes. ("Friendly" was used to describe American Indians who sought peace with whites; those who refused to make peace were known as "hostiles.") Nearly one hundred Cheyenne families had been wiped out.

The surviving bands went on a quest for revenge, killing as many whites as they could and stealing and destroying their property. The army did not have the power to stop the rampage. The horrors of the massacre and the tales of the Cheyenne's subsequent success in fighting the whites spread among many Indians a desire for all-out war with the white invaders.

There was still a considerable number of Lakota who wanted to make peace, and these gathered at Fort Sully in October 1865 to sign treaties promising to keep the peace and stay clear of the routes used by settlers. In exchange, the U.S. government would provide annuities.

Sitting Bull and many other Hunkpapa stayed away from this meeting and continued to attack army posts. In the summer of 1866, their hostility increased when the army began building

In the Fetterman Massacre, Red Cloud led his warriors to victory over a unit of U.S. cavalry soldiers.

Fort Buford in the very heart of Hunkpapa territory. Warriors attacked the men who were building the fort as well as any travelers they came across.

While Sitting Bull was occupied with Fort Buford, the Oglala under Red Cloud were fighting against the forts being built along the Bozeman Trail. This new route brought miners through the western part of Lakota territory to the gold mines of Montana Territory. On December 21, a small war party lured Captain William J. Fetterman and eighty-one men into an ambush. Every soldier was killed. This incident became known among whites as the Fetterman Massacre, and among the Lakota as the Hundred-Soldiers-Killed Fight. Sitting Bull's nephew White Bull was present at this fight, as was a young Oglala warrior who was just beginning to make his mark on history—Crazy Horse.

An account of this fight was narrated in 1931 to poet John G. Neihardt by Black Elk, an Oglala holy man who was three years old at the time of the battle:

I had never seen a Wasichu then, and did not know what one looked like; but every one was saying that the Wasichus were coming and that they were going to take our country and rub us all out and that we should all have to die fighting. It was the Wasichus who got rubbed out in that battle, and all the people were talking about it for a long while; but a hundred Wasichus was not much if there were others and others without number where those came from.

When I was older, I learned what the fighting was about that winter and the next summer. Up on the Madison Fork the Wasichus had found much of the yellow metal that they worship and that makes them crazy, and they wanted to have a road up through our country to the place where the yellow metal was; but my people did not want the road. It would scare the bison and make them go away, and also it would let the other Wasichus come in like a river. They told us that they wanted only to use a little land, as much as a wagon would take between the wheels; but our people knew better. And when you look about you now, you can see what it was they wanted.

Throughout the winter, Sitting Bull and his followers held Fort Buford in a state of siege. The warriors surrounded the fort, ensuring that the soldiers within could not venture out for supplies or communicate with anyone. Reinforcements arrived in the spring, but the Lakota continued their attacks. According to the surgeon who was stationed at the fort, "Messages from Sitting Bull continued to be received from time to time, announcing that at no distant day Fort Buford was to be destroyed from the face of the earth."

"Fort Buford was to be destroyed from the face of the earth."

Both Sitting Bull and Red Cloud continued to harass the forts throughout 1867. In 1868, the U.S. government renewed its attempts to make peace with the Plains tribes in hopes that the Indians would stay clear of the roads and the new railroads that cut through their territory. A new Fort Laramie Treaty was drawn up. According to its terms, the Lakota would eventually be confined to the Great Sioux Reservation, which would comprise the western half of what is now the state of South Dakota. This was one of the many terms of the treaty that the Lakota could not comprehend. Their way of life depended on their ability to roam over vast expanses in search of buffalo herds. It was not explained that the Lakota would be expected to give up their lives as roaming hunters and to settle down and farm like the whites. Neither was it explained that they would be expected to send their children to American schools that would teach them to speak and act like whites and practice Christianity.

Red Cloud and other Oglala and Miniconjou chiefs signed the treaty as soon as the government agreed to abandon the Bozeman Trail. But Sitting Bull could not be so easily won because the whites had no intention of leaving his territory. Knowing that Sitting Bull had no interest in speaking to government agents, in whom he had no trust, the government sent a representative who had already earned the respect of many American Indians. Pierre-Jean De Smet was a *Jesuit missionary* who genuinely wanted peace. The Sioux saw in this holy man a wasichu who could be trusted, and even Sitting Bull agreed to meet him.

Father De Smet was given a warm welcome when he arrived at Sitting Bull's camp on June 19, 1868. The chiefs spoke with him about their desire for peace. Sitting Bull told the priest that nothing would make him happier than to make peace with the whites, but this could not happen as long as there were forts in his homeland and the whites continued to desire his land.

On July 2, the Fort Laramie Treaty was read to a gathering of Hunkpapa, Blackfeet, and Yanktonai at Fort Rice. Sitting Bull would not attend, having no faith that the treaty would meet his demands. He sent Gall, a war chief and close friend, to hear what the whites had to say.

Each of the twenty chiefs present was expected to make a speech. Gall was the first to speak, and he laid out his terms. It is clear that he did not understand that the terms of **"The whites ruin our country."** the treaty had already been written out and that all he could do was sign and accept the treaty as it was. Gall told the treaty commission, "The whites ruin our country. If we make peace, the military posts on this river must be removed and the steamboats stopped from coming up here."

Of course, the government had no intention of meeting his demands, but Gall did not know that when he signed the Fort Laramie Treaty of 1868. He certainly did not suspect that he had agreed that his people would live on a reservation and give up their customs. And although the twenty signatories were seen by the U.S. government as representatives of all members of their tribes, Sitting Bull did not see it that way. He was far from ready to give up his fight against the intrusions into his homeland.

After the signing of the Fort Laramie treaty, *agencies* began to spring up throughout the Lakota territory. Agencies were administrative centers for the reservation, where government agents gave the Indians the supplies promised them under treaty and did their best to keep the Indians under control. As the "friendly" Lakota moved to the agencies, the rift grew deeper between those Lakota who wanted to meet the demands of the U.S. government in exchange for peace and those who refused to make any concessions.

Sitting Bull's uncle Four Horns, one of the four shirt-wearers and a highly respected leader, saw the need to unite all the Lakota who wanted to avoid the agencies and continue to follow the buffalo. At that time, about one-third of the Lakota would follow him. If they were going to fight off the encroachment of the whites, they would need to act as one. And so he proposed that for the first time in the history of the Lakota there should be a single leader for all the bands and tribes. And his nomination for the position of supreme chief of the Lakota was Sitting Bull.

Although his proposal ran counter to the traditional political structure, in which each band acted independently, many saw the need for unity in the face of the wasichus. Sitting Bull was a natural choice for the role. During his eleven years as a war chief, he had proven to be a tireless warrior in the fight against encroachment by the whites in his country. His wisdom and spiritual strength, combined with his unwavering opposition to entering into agreements with whites, made him the perfect leader for the Lakota who saw life on a reservation as no better than death.

In 1869, the tribes met to vote on Sitting Bull's nomination. Representatives of every tribe voiced their support for Sitting Bull, and Four Horns said to Sitting Bull, "For your bravery on the battlefields and as the greatest warrior of our bands, we have elected you as our war chief, leader of the entire Sioux nation. When you tell us to fight, we shall fight, when you tell us to make peace, we shall make peace." A ceremony was then held to mark his elevation to supreme chief.

"When you tell us to fight, we shall fight."

By this time, Red Cloud had given up his fight with the whites because he saw the move to the reservation as inevitable. He believed that the best thing he could do for his people was to make their lives there comfortable and to help them hold on to as much of their traditional way of life as possible. He took provisions from the agencies and spent much of his time there, but in the warm months he led his people out of the agency to pursue the buffalo.

Crazy Horse, like Sitting Bull, passionately resisted the white advance.

Now that Red Cloud had given up the fight, the Oglala who refused to move to an agency rallied behind Crazy Horse. A fierce warrior, Crazy Horse shared Sitting Bull's determination never to give up his land or his way of life.

Around 1870, Sitting Bull's family life went through many changes. First, he adopted another brother—twenty-one-year-old Frank Grouard, who was being held captive by the Hunkpapa. Grouard was a Mormon who left his home at the age of fifteen to seek adventure in the northern Plains. Sitting Bull would eventually regret taking Grouard into his home. Unlike Jumping Bull, Grouard would not remain loyal to his adopted brother. In 1873, after a quarrel with Sitting Bull, he went to live with the Oglala and became a close friend of Crazy Horse. But he would eventually leave the Lakota and work for the army, where he would use his knowledge of the Lakota against them.

Soon Sitting Bull found himself without a wife. A few years earlier, the hostility between his two wives became so disruptive that he ended his marriage to Snow-on-Her. Then, in 1871, Red Woman died. Although his sister Good Feather and his mother helped take care of his three children, he needed a new wife. He married a woman named Four Robes, and when her widowed sister, Seen-by-the-Nation, expressed a desire to live with them, Sitting Bull married her too. These women got along very well, and Sitting Bull never again had the problems that he had endured with his previous wives.

CHAPTER 5

ALL-OUT WAR

One of Sitting Bull's first challenges as supreme chief of the Lakota was a new intrusion into his homeland. A railroad was being built through the Yellowstone Valley, a favorite hunting area that had recently been won from the Crow. This would mean a new flood of whites into the region, and the trains would scare off the buffalo herds that could often be found in the valley.

The government tried to appease the Indians by offering them food. This was tempting to the Lakota, whose hunting grounds were becoming less bountiful because of the impact of the whites. Many bands gathered at the agencies during harsh winters, when the food stores were low. In spring, they resumed hunting and warfare, against the whites as well as enemy tribes.

In the summer of 1872, the Lakota fought their first battle against the railroad. After a Sun

*By the time Sitting Bull became chief, the railroads
were a serious threat to the Lakota way of life.*

Dance at which thousands of Lakota had gathered, the assembled bands decided to attack the
Crow. About 1,000 warriors were heading for
Crow territory when they spotted a group of railroad *surveyors* escorted by 500 soldiers.

In the ensuing Battle of Arrow Creek,
Sitting Bull gave an unusually dangerous
demonstration of his bravery. He sat on the
ground in view of the soldiers and asked if anyone would like to smoke his pipe with him. White
Bull and three others joined Sitting Bull as he
calmly filled and lit the pipe. White Bull later
recalled, "We others wasted no time. Our hearts

beat rapidly, and we smoked as fast as we could. All around us the bullets were kicking up the dust, and we could hear bullets whining overhead. But Sitting Bull was not afraid. He just sat there quietly, looking around as if he were at home in his tent, and smoked peacefully." This act of bravery strengthened Sitting Bull's reputation as the fearless leader of the Lakota.

"But Sitting Bull was not afraid. He just sat there quietly."

The Battle of Arrow Creek ended with only a few casualties on each side, but it showed that the Indians would not allow a railroad to pass through their land in exchange for some food from the government.

Soon after the battle, Sitting Bull received word that Gall and a small group of warriors had encountered another military expedition, with about 600 soldiers. Although greatly outnumbered, Gall's men fired on the soldiers' camp and continued to skirmish with them for a few days until Sitting Bull arrived with reinforcements. The gathering of Lakota was still no match for the large unit of soldiers, and they succeeded in killing only a few. But both Gall and Sitting Bull used the opportunity to issue a warning that they would gather their people together to kill any soldier or worker who tried to further the progress of the railroad.

The advance of whites into the Black Hills angered the Lakota.

In 1873, economic conditions in the United States, rather than Lakota warfare, halted construction of the railroad. But the battles against the railroad convinced the U.S. government that Sitting Bull was a leader to be reckoned with and that he would not agree to any treaty that gave whites the rights to any part of his homeland.

However, there was soon new cause for interest in the Lakota territory: rumors of gold in the Black Hills. The Black Hills were the most beloved part of the Lakota territory. They were considered a sacred place where the Lakota held important ceremonies. The hills were also home to bountiful game, and the trees that grew there were sought after for tepee poles. The Lakota tried to keep out any miners who made their way to the sacred hills, but as interest increased in the gold rumored to be there, the government intervened.

In 1874, General George Armstrong Custer led an expedition into the Black Hills. His report that the hills held a wealth of gold started a rush of miners into the area. This intrusion into the Black Hills was in violation of the Treaty of 1868, and the Lakota demanded that the government keep miners away. The government responded by sending a commission to buy the Black Hills.

The Lakota were invited to the Red Cloud Agency to work out an agreement. Sitting Bull and Crazy Horse refused to go, but Little-Big-Man, a member of Crazy Horse's camp, led a charge of warriors to the council, dressed for battle and shooting rifles in the air. Little-Big-Man threatened to shoot anyone who agreed to sign a treaty. The Lakota informed the commission that they had no intention of giving up the Black Hills. A man named White Ghost said, "You have driven away our game and our means of livelihood out of the country, until now we have nothing left that is valuable except the hills that you ask us to give up. . . . The earth is full of minerals of all kinds, and on the earth the ground is covered with forests of heavy pine, and when we give these up to the Great Father we know that we give up the last thing that is valuable either to us or the white people."

Since diplomacy failed, the government resorted to force. The Sioux were now seen as a hostile tribe that was standing in the way of progress, and the only way for the United States to get their land was by going to war. On December 6, 1875, the Indian agents were ordered to inform all nonreservation Sioux to report to an agency by January 31, 1876. On February 1, the War Department would be responsible for dealing with any Sioux who had not gone to a reservation.

When couriers arrived in the winter camps of the hunting bands and delivered the news, the Indians did not understand why they were being summoned or that failing to appear would result in war. Even if they had wanted to comply, the heavy snow would have made it impossible to move their camps. Sitting Bull, probably thinking that he was being invited to another treaty council, replied to a courier that he might come to the agency in the spring. Crazy Horse gave a similar response.

The first strike in the war against the Sioux took place on March 17, 1876, at a camp on the Powder River, which was mistaken for Crazy Horse's camp. The camp was made up of Northern

Cheyenne, Oglala, and Miniconjou. As the Indians slept, troops under General George Crook charged into the camp and opened fire on the tepees. As women and children ran for safety, the men fought back, killing four soldiers. Only two Indians were killed, but the soldiers burned their possessions, leaving them in the bitter cold with no homes, no buffalo robes to keep them warm, and little food. The troops stole the horses from the camp, but that night the Indians crept into the soldiers' camp and reclaimed their horses.

These cold, hungry Indians traveled 60 miles (96.5 km) through the snow to reach Sitting Bull's village. Sitting Bull and his people gave them food and clothing and made room for them in their homes. The Hunkpapa were stunned by the story they heard about the attack on the Powder River. And Sitting Bull was especially heartbroken to learn that the soldiers had been led to the camp by his adopted brother, Frank Grouard, who was serving as a scout for the army.

Sitting Bull was now prepared for an all-out war with the whites. He declared, "We are an island of Indians in a lake of whites. We must stand together, or they will rub us out separately. These soldiers have come shooting; they want war. All right, we'll give it to them!"

As word of the attack spread to the hunting bands, they made their way to Sitting Bull's camp, planning to unite against further attacks. Throughout the spring, this group of about 3,000 Lakota and Cheyenne traveled together, following the buffalo. They sometimes spotted soldiers looking for the Indians, and they tried to avoid them, wanting to fight only when necessary.

"These soldiers have come shooting; they want war. All right, we'll give it to them!"

In May, Sitting Bull felt compelled to go to the top of a *butte* and await a vision. After praying, he fell asleep and saw a dust storm coming from the east and approaching a white cloud that looked like an Indian village. The storm charged toward the cloud, and behind the storm was an enormous army. As the two forces met, there was thunder and lightning. The dust cloud disappeared, and the white cloud floated off. Sitting Bull explained that this meant that the soldiers would come to attack, but that the Indians would defeat them.

In the weeks that followed, Sitting Bull said many prayers for the well-being of the people, and he held a Sun Dance so that he could make sacrifices to Wakantanka. First he made an offering of his flesh. After purifying himself in a sweat lodge and performing a pipe ceremony, Sitting Bull sat against the pole around which the Sun Dance would be performed. Then Jumping Bull inserted an awl through the skin near Sitting Bull's wrist, lifted the skin, and cut off a small piece. He repeated this all the way up the arm and then did the same on the other arm, until 100 pieces of flesh had been removed. All the while, Sitting Bull cried out in prayer to Wakantanka.

Sitting Bull then performed the Sun Dance and had another vision. He saw a huge army approaching a village, but the soldiers were all upside down. He heard a voice tell him that all of the soldiers would be killed but that the Indians should not take weapons or possessions from the dead.

Sitting Bull told the people, "These dead soldiers who are coming are the gifts of [Wakantanka]. Kill them, but do not take their guns or horses. Do not touch the spoils. If you set your hearts upon the goods of the white man, it will prove a curse to this nation."

"If you set your hearts upon the goods of the white man, it will prove a curse to this nation."

After the Sun Dance, the Cheyenne and Sioux camp moved to Reno Creek, between the Rosebud and Little Bighorn rivers. Scouts were on the lookout for the soldiers Sitting Bull had seen in his visions, and on June 16, 1876, Cheyenne scouts rode into camp reporting swarms of soldiers along the Rosebud. The next morning, about 1,000 warriors prepared for battle and made for the Rosebud.

As they approached General Crook's troops, the warriors first encountered their Crow scouts, who were looking for the Sioux camp. Fighting broke out between these traditional enemies, and soon Crook's troops charged into the battle. Sitting Bull was not able to fight because of the wounds on his arm, but he rode among his men, urging them to be brave.

The fighting went on for most of the day. The Indians were outnumbered, but they were tireless, and their experiences with battling whites made them stronger opponents than they had been in past battles with the army. In the late afternoon, the Sioux and Cheyenne carried off their dead and returned to their camp. The soldiers did not attempt to follow. They had expected to launch a surprise attack, but instead the Indians had surprised them. They were so stunned by the number of warriors and by their skill and tenacity that they returned to the safety of their fort. General Crook would not attempt another attack until he had received large numbers of reinforcements.

In the village of the Sioux and Cheyenne there was mourning for the dead. The camp was then moved to the valley of the Little Bighorn River, known to the Lakota as the Greasy Grass. There the Indians feasted and celebrated their victory for several days. During the festivities they were joined by Sioux who had left the agency for the summer to hunt. Their arrival raised the population of the camp on the Little Bighorn to 7,000, making the people even more confident in their ability to fight off the wasichus. Sitting Bull was still waiting for the soldiers he had seen in his vision; the soldiers who would attack the camp and be completely wiped out.

The afternoon of June 25 began as a quiet day in the village. Some people found shady spots to rest while others cooled off in the river. Many of the women were out digging for turnips, and some of the men tended to the horses. Suddenly the peace was shattered by cries that soldiers had been spotted at the site of the camp where they had fought General Crook. It would not be long before the soldiers followed the trail from there to the camp on the Little Bighorn.

The soldiers they saw were the Seventh Cavalry, led by General Custer, whom the Indians knew as Long Hair. As 750 soldiers rode toward the village, their horses kicked up a huge dust cloud, like the one Sitting Bull saw in his vision.

General Custer was a fierce, but reckless, soldier.

The men hurriedly prepared for battle, and the women and children fled the village. Sitting Bull was concerned about his family, which had grown to include three-week-old twin sons. He took his elderly mother and one of his sisters into the hills while his wives helped the children make their escape. Some of the women and children did not make it out of the village. Gall's two wives and three children were killed by scouts who rode ahead of the cavalry.

By the time Sitting Bull and his nephews returned to his tepee to grab their weapons, gunfire was blasting through the village. Sitting Bull gave One Bull the shield that his father had given him, and the three men joined the fighting.

The Indians were given several advantages by General Custer. His original plan had been to let his men rest overnight. Then he would send out scouts to find the village, and he could work out a strategy to overtake the Indians. However, on June 25 he spotted some Indians and was afraid that Sitting Bull would be warned of his advance. This could result in a replay of the Battle of the Rosebud. So he decided to push his men on until they found the Indians and then start fighting.

Also, he abandoned the strategy that had been set forth by General Alfred Terry, who was in command of this campaign against Sitting Bull. Custer was supposed to attack the village from the south while troops under General Terry and General John Gibbon approached the village from the north, so that the Indians would be attacked from two sides. General Terry had no idea of the enormous size of the village. He believed that if the troops approached from two directions, they would cut off the escape route of the Indians trying to flee Custer. But when Custer thought that he had been discovered by Sioux scouts, he decided not to waste time looping around to attack from the south. He stormed directly into the village, without allowing General Gibbon time to get there.

Custer divided the cavalry into three battalions. One of these, led by Captain Frederick Benteen, and another, under Major Marcus Reno, were sent to attack the village farther upstream while Custer's troops made a direct attack. When Custer arrived at the village, there were only 210 men with him.

As predicted in Sitting Bull's vision, the Indians wiped out Custer's entire battalion. When Reno and Benteen arrived they were overwhelmed by the warriors. They knew that they could not defeat the Indians. Now they only hoped to save their own lives. The next day, after many of these soldiers had been killed or wounded, Sitting Bull told his warriors to end the fighting and let the surviving soldiers go.

Surrounded by Indian warriors, Custer and his men are overwhelmed.

The joy over this victory was dampened by the losses among the Sioux. And Sitting Bull was further saddened that his people had not heeded the warning he had received in his vision. They had not been able to overcome the temptation to take weapons and other belongings from the fallen soldiers. He feared that this would doom them to dependence on the whites.

CHAPTER 6

SURRENDER

When word of the Indians' victory over the army reached Washington, it cemented the desire of the U.S. government and many of its citizens to wipe out the Sioux once and for all. The first Sioux to be punished were those who had not taken part in the fighting. The Sioux reservations were put under military control. The Indians who lived there became prisoners of war, and their guns and horses were *confiscated.* Then the agency Indians were forced into signing away the Black Hills and the valley of the Powder River.

Reinforcements were sent to fight the hunting bands and get them to join the reservation Sioux as prisoners of war. In October 1876, Sitting Bull and his people encountered Colonel Nelson A. Miles, who had come in search of him. Sitting Bull was interested only in feeding his people. He would fight the whites when attacked, but he still

▲ 72 ▲

*After the Battle of Little Bighorn, Sitting Bull
still hoped for a return to peace.*

had hope that they would leave his people to hunt and get on with their lives.

So when Miles's troops approached the camp, Sitting Bull asked two men to ride out under a white flag to arrange a meeting. Miles agreed, and Sitting Bull and Miles met, unarmed, each accompanied by a small group of supporters, while the armed soldiers and warriors looked on from a distance. Miles was wearing a long coat trimmed with bear fur, and he would thereafter be known as Bear Coat.

Sitting Bull told Miles what he had told every other delegation he had met with, that he wanted the whites to leave his country and leave his people in peace. But Miles warned that if Sitting Bull and his followers did not surrender immediately, he would attack. Fighting broke out and the Indians tried to get away. By now, some of the bands that had joined with Sitting Bull saw surrender as their only means of survival. Many of the Miniconjou and Sans Arc surrendered. Miles took five prisoners and instructed the rest to turn themselves in at the Cheyenne River Agency. They did not turn themselves in, but the lack of resolve among his followers discouraged Sitting Bull.

Even more bands were ready to surrender in the harsh winter ahead. The Sioux and their enemies usually refrained from fighting in the winter, but the army did not stop. The extreme weather

The destruction of the buffalo herds devastated the Plains Indian tribes. In this photo, buffalo skulls have been piled into a gigantic pyramid.

would have made it difficult for the Sioux in the best of times, but the frequent attacks and the presence of soldiers in the hunting grounds made the winter almost unbearable. Attacks on villages usually resulted in the destruction of the Indians' possessions, so they were left with little to eat, a shortage of tepees, and few buffalo robes to protect them from the bitter cold.

Many believed that the only alternative to surrender was starving or freezing to death, so numerous bands turned themselves in at the agencies. In May, after fighting valiantly through the winter, even Crazy Horse was driven to surrender. Many Sioux had fled the army by crossing into Canada, and Sitting Bull thought that his people might have a chance to live free there. So in May 1877, Sitting Bull and about 1,000 people followed their lead and left the United States.

Soon after their arrival in what is now the province of Saskatchewan, the Sioux were approached by seven members of the North-West Mounted Police. Sitting Bull met with Major James M. Walsh, who told the chief that his people were welcome to stay in Canada as long as they obeyed Canadian laws. This would mean refraining from fighting with other tribes and stealing horses. Also, because Canada did not want to have diplomatic troubles with the United States, he did not want any Indians living in Canada to return to the United States and cause trouble there. Anyone who did so would not be welcome to return to Canada.

Sitting Bull respected Walsh's bravery in entering the camp with only six men, and his demands were reasonable. He felt that this was a white man he could trust. But he also feared that there was no way to keep young men from fighting and stealing.

Although the Canadians said that the Sioux were welcome, they knew that their presence would cause friction, both with Canadian tribes and with the United States. Many of the tribes that lived in the area, such as the Blackfeet, Blood, and Cree, were enemies of the Sioux, and the Canadians feared that intertribal warfare would erupt. And hostilities seemed inevitable as they would be competing for limited sources of food.

The buffalo population of the Great Plains had been decreasing since the arrival of whites. The trade in buffalo hides and tongues, which were considered a delicacy, resulted in a drastic reduction in their numbers. The intrusion of railroads and towns interfered with the buffalo's migration in search of food. And many buffalo were killed for the sole purpose of destroying the Indians' source of food. By the time of Sitting Bull's arrival in Canada, the Indians who lived there were struggling to retain their traditional hunting lifestyle in the face of the disappearance of the buffalo. They were not happy to have newcomers competing for the same shrinking resources.

Rumors that the Sioux were strengthening themselves for further warfare in the United States led the U.S. government to demand that Canada keep the Sioux confined on a reservation.

Canadian officials explained that the Sioux would probably give up if they were allowed to keep their horses and guns, but the U.S. government wanted nothing short of unconditional surrender.

In October 1877, Walsh convinced Sitting Bull to meet with a commission led by General Terry. The commission tried to persuade Sitting Bull to join the other Lakota on a reservation, but Sitting Bull stated that his people had been treated very poorly in the United States and that they would remain in Canada.

As Sitting Bull spoke to the commission, he did not yet know the fate that had befallen his friend Crazy Horse. The followers of Crazy Horse could not adjust to life at the agency, and they caused trouble for the agents. Crazy Horse had been arrested, and on September 7, he was stabbed during a struggle with the guards.

Soon after, the Indians who lived at the Red Cloud and Spotted Tail agencies were forced to move. During the trip to the new agency, many of Crazy Horse's former followers chose a new destination and headed for Canada to find Sitting Bull. About 2,000 people settled near Sitting Bull in the spring of 1878.

The buffalo hunt sometimes brought the Sioux back into the United States. This often led to the kind of trouble that Walsh had warned Sitting Bull to avoid. Young men would sometimes steal from whites or other tribes or kill livestock out of desperation. During a hunt in July 1879, Sitting Bull and about 600 followers were discovered by Bear Coat Miles's troops. The ensuing battle strengthened the desire of the U.S. government to get the Sioux out of Canada and onto a reservation.

Sitting Bull's obstinate resistance to surrendering was well known, so Canadian officials concentrated their attempts on other chiefs. Gradually, most of the Sioux who had followed Sitting Bull to Canada were convinced that going to an agency was the only way to ensure the survival of their families. Sitting Bull lost many of his longtime comrades, including Gall and Jumping Bull. White Bull had already surrendered with his band.

This was an increasingly bewildering time for Sitting Bull. More and more Lakota were leaving Canada. Most of the young men surrendered, which made it difficult to supply food for the people who remained. In spite of his insistence on remaining a hunter, he knew that his children might face starvation. His family was still growing; a daughter, Standing Holy, was born in 1878, and twin sons were born in 1880. His responsibility to his wives, his children, and his mother, as well as the others who still looked to him for guidance, weighed heavily on him. His resistance to surrender began to weaken. In 1880 he sent One Bull to Fort Buford to ask about the conditions of surrender, and in April 1881 he sent him to see how the Sioux were being treated at the agencies. He exasperated Canadian officials by saying that he would surrender but then changing his mind.

After three years in Canada, Sitting Bull could hold out no longer. On July 19, 1881, he arrived at Fort Buford with nearly 200 followers. The next day, a meeting was held between the officials of Fort Buford and Sitting Bull. David H. Brotherton, the commander of Fort Buford, assured Sitting Bull that he would live among his people at Standing Rock Agency.

Sitting Bull motioned to his five-year-old son Crow Foot, who handed his father's rifle to Brotherton as a sign of surrender. Sitting Bull then said:

> I surrender this rifle to you through my young son, whom I now desire to teach in this manner that he has become a friend of the Americans. I wish him to learn the habits of the whites and to be educated as their sons are educated. I wish it to be remembered that I was the last man of my tribe to surrender my rifle. This boy has given it to you, and he now wants to know how he is going to make a living.

Realizing that his situation was hopeless, Sitting Bull surrendered himself and briefly embraced white ways. In this photo, Sitting Bull sits with several generals and a general's wife.

In spite of these assurances that Sitting Bull was going to live the way he was expected, he was viewed as a threat. It was feared that he would stir up the residents of Standing Rock, so Brotherton's promise that he would live there was broken. After spending a few weeks at Standing Rock, during which he was comforted by visiting with family and friends, Sitting Bull and the people who entered Fort Buford with him were transported to Fort Randall, where they would remain for nearly two years. After all his efforts to remain free, he had ended up a prisoner, kept out of contact with his people. After an active life as a hunter and warrior, he was left to sit idly and collect rations from the government.

CHAPTER 7

A LIVING LEGEND

In May 1883, Sitting Bull and the others who were held at Fort Randall were returned to Standing Rock, where they would be taught to farm and otherwise act like white Americans. When Sitting Bull arrived, he found that his standing as a leader of his people did not hold any value with Standing Rock's Indian agent, James McLaughlin. The only way to gain a position of authority was to win the favor of the agent by embracing the ways of the whites and encouraging others to do the same. In McLaughlin's eyes, the representative of the Hunkpapa was Gall, who had taken to dressing like a white man and did what he could to gain favor with the agent. Sitting Bull, on the other hand, was seen as a troublemaker, and McLaughlin sought to undermine his authority among his people by spreading rumors and refusing to acknowledge his standing as a chief. Sitting Bull's mood was worsened by a prophecy of his own death. Soon after his arrival at Standing Rock, while climbing a hill near his new home, he heard a voice. As he looked around he spotted a meadowlark, a bird that was known for its ability to communicate with the Sioux. It told Sitting Bull something that would haunt him for the rest of his life: "Lakotas will kill you."

"Lakotas will kill you."

A year after his arrival, Sitting Bull settled on a plot of land along the Grand River, not far from the spot on which he had been born. There he began his efforts to make a living as a farmer, as all Indians were encouraged to do. He and his family were very successful at this new endeavor. And he sent his children to a school run by Congregational missionaries, because he believed it was important for the children to know how to read and write if they were going to succeed in this new life.

After fifty-two years of almost constant travel, Sitting Bull could not be content to live the life of a farmer. He wanted to see the cities of the whites and understand their ways. For years he had been dealing with whites at forts and trading posts, or with the soldiers who made their way through his country, but it was not until he surrendered that he got a glimpse of the way they lived in their cities.

After his surrender at Fort Buford in 1881, Sitting Bull was transported down the Missouri River to the Standing Rock Agency. The boat stopped at the city of Bismarck. The people of the city thronged to see the living legend who had defeated Custer and been the object of such fear and hatred among the citizens, government, and military of the United States. Now that the Lakota no longer posed a threat, the whites' fear of Sitting Bull had turned to curiosity and admiration.

The aging chief had a desire to see more of the whites' ways. He had his chance in September 1883, when Bismarck held a celebration to mark its selection as capital of the Dakota territory. A delegation of Lakota were invited to represent the native Dakotans. Sitting Bull spoke before the gathering and was introduced to the governor. The following year he and one of his wives and One Bull accompanied McLaughlin on a trip to St. Paul. Sitting Bull was given tours of businesses and government offices, and was impressed by the technology that was fueling the rapid growth of industry in the United States.

The popularity of Sitting Bull attracted the attention of a hotel owner in St. Paul who wanted to take Sitting Bull on the road and have him appear before audiences in fifteen cities. The Sitting Bull Combination opened in New York City on September 15, 1884. The show was intended to show a slice of Sioux life. Sitting Bull and a small group of Lakota sat on stage near a tepee and pretended to go about their daily routine, the women preparing food while the men smoked. A narrator described their traditional lifestyle. A Lakota who had learned to speak English at boarding school attended a performance in Philadelphia and recalled that Sitting Bull addressed the audience about his desire to stay at peace with the whites. But when his speech was translated for the audience, it turned into an account of the battle with Custer.

Another tour followed in 1885, this time with Buffalo Bill's Wild West Show. William "Buffalo Bill" Cody had worked as an army scout and buffalo hunter on the plains and had even scouted for General Crook during his pursuit of Sitting Bull in 1876. Buffalo Bill had turned showman and brought to audiences a spectacle of frontier life in the West, complete with cowboys, Indians, and sharpshooters. Sitting Bull joined the show on a tour of the United States and Canada. He became close friends with Buffalo Bill and the expert marksman, Annie Oakley, whom he named Little Sure Shot.

Although Sitting Bull was intrigued by the innovations of the whites, he was disgusted by the disparity between rich and poor. The Lakota prided themselves on sharing their wealth with others

In 1876, Sitting Bull became a star attraction of the Buffalo Bill Wild West Show. Here, Sitting Bull poses with Buffalo Bill Cody.

A poster from Buffalo Bill's Wild West Show

and always took care of those who could not support their families. Now he was confronted with children begging in the street. According to Annie Oakley, much of his earnings "went into the pockets of small, ragged boys. Nor could he understand how so much wealth could go brushing by, unmindful of the poor."

He later told a missionary on the reservation, "The farther my people keep away from the whites, the better I shall be satisfied. The white people are wicked and I don't want my women to become as the white women I have seen have lived. I want you to teach my people to read and write but they must not become white people in their ways; it is too bad a life, I could not let them do it. . . . I would rather die an Indian than live a white man."

The Buffalo Bill tour was followed by serious troubles on the Great Sioux Reservation. When the reservation was created under the treaty of 1868, the land was undesirable to white settlers. But now settlers were anxious to obtain farmland on the Plains, and the reservation was a tempting piece of real estate. The General Allotment Act of 1887 served a dual purpose: to encourage the Indians to live more like whites by giving each family a plot of land, and to open land to white settlers by selling any reservation lands that were left after allotments had been distributed. In the case of the Great Sioux Reservation, this would mean that 9 million acres (3.6 million hectares) would be lost.

The Sioux Act of 1888 followed. This would divide the Great Sioux Reservation into six small reservations, which would then be divided into allotments. The remaining 9 million acres (3.6 million hectares) would be sold for fifty cents an acre (0.4 hectares). This proposal infuriated the Sioux, who had already seen so much of their land disappear. Sitting Bull had tried to be cooperative

"I would rather die an Indian than live a white man."

Sitting Bull remained proud of his Indian ways.

with the Indian agent and had worked hard to earn his living from farming, but the idea of individual ownership of property ran counter to Sioux tradition. Bands had always worked together for the good of all. Now people were expected to work only for their own family.

In July, a commission arrived on the reservation to obtain the signatures of three-quarters of the adult males, which would be necessary to pass the law. Sitting Bull spoke out against this act, but the Sioux did not need much convincing. No one wanted to sign, and after a month of trying to persuade them, the commission knew their attempts were futile. It was decided that the Sioux should send representatives to Washington, D.C., to work out a resolution. Sitting Bull and sixty other chiefs arrived in October.

The chiefs enjoyed their tour of the capital and met President Grover Cleveland, but no agreement was reached. Another proposal was soon brought before the Sioux. The Sioux Act of 1889 raised the price of the land to be sold. Once again, the people strongly opposed the sale of their land, but this time the commission worked hard to gain favor with the people and cause divisions among the leadership. McLaughlin exerted his influence over Gall and the other chiefs who were always eager to remain in good standing with the agent. Sitting Bull tried to stop the men from signing, first with impassioned speeches and then with a desperate attempt to break up the proceedings by leading a charge of twenty warriors onto the scene of the signing. But the commission obtained all the signatures it needed.

The loss of a major part of the reservation's land was followed by more hardships. First, the government cut back on the beef rations that it supplied the Sioux. Then came the winter of 1889–1890, when a bad crop the previous summer combined with the reduced beef rations led to widespread hunger, and many Indians fell victim to epidemics of measles, influenza, and whooping cough. Summer brought no reprieve from the suffering as the crops were devastated by drought.

In these desperate times, the Lakota were receptive to a new religious movement that was bringing hope to American Indian communities. Wovoka, a Paiute holy man in Nevada, prophesied a rebirth of the world. The buffalo would be restored, the earth would provide abundance for the Indians, and they would be reunited with friends and family who had died. All tribes would live in peace, and there would be no white people. The only people to survive this great change would be those who practiced the Ghost Dance.

Black Elk, who participated in a Ghost Dance that Kicking Bear held near Wounded Knee Creek, described the scene:

Before we started dancing next day, Kicking Bear offered a prayer, saying: "Father, Great Spirit, behold these people! They shall go forth today to see their relatives, and yonder they shall be happy, day after day, and their happiness will not end.

Then we began dancing, and most of the people wailed and cried as they danced, holding hands in a circle; but some of them laughed with happiness. Now and then some one would fall down like dead, and others would go staggering around and panting before they would fall. While they were lying there like dead they were having visions, and we kept on dancing and singing, and many were crying for the old way of living and that the old religion might be with them again.

In October, Sitting Bull invited Kicking Bear to Standing Rock. Kicking Bear was a Miniconjou who had gone to Nevada to learn about the Ghost Dance religion from Wovoka. By this time, the religion had caught on at many reservations, including the Pine Ridge, Rosebud, and Cheyenne River reservations of the Sioux. The agents and missionaries were frightened by this religion. Converting Indians to Christianity was an important part of the "civilization" process through which the Indians would lose their tribal identity. Now the Indians were caught up in a religious movement that united tribes all over the country. The sight of Indians dancing frantically and then falling into a trancelike state as visions came to them was alarming, as was their desire for a world without whites. Agents and nearby settlers feared that the movement would lead to an Indian uprising.

Sitting Bull brought this fear to Standing Rock when he began to hold Ghost Dances. McLaughlin was worried about the effect that the religion would have at his agency. He was not reassured by the opinion of a teacher on the reservation who wrote, "The Indians seem to be very peaceably inclined, and I do not apprehend any trouble. . . . The Indians have been told that soldiers are coming down here, and are badly frightened . . . I am positive that no trouble need be apprehended from Sitting Bull and his followers, unless they are forced to defend themselves." McLaughlin wrote to the Bureau of Indian Affairs requesting permission to arrest Sitting Bull and send him to military prison. His request was denied.

> "I am positive that no trouble need be apprehended from Sitting Bull."

Meanwhile, the agents at the other Sioux reservations feared they no longer had any control over the Indians. The Department of War was given authority to deal with the Ghost Dancers, and troops were sent to Pine Ridge and Rosebud.

McLaughlin wanted to avoid a military presence at Standing Rock, so he decided that he should handle Sitting Bull himself. He would wait until the winter snow halted the dancing and then have the Indian police arrest him. He believed that the dancers would be less likely to rebel if Sitting Bull were arrested by Lakotas.

However, before the first snow fell, Sitting Bull's friend Buffalo Bill arrived at Fort Yates and presented its commander, Colonel William Drum, with orders from General "Bear Coat" Miles, who still had not lost interest in Sitting Bull. Buffalo Bill was to bring Sitting Bull to the fort, and Drum and his men were to provide assistance.

McLaughlin sent a telegram to the Indian Office, explaining that this scenario could lead to violence. President Benjamin Harrison agreed and called off the plan. However, Miles would not be deterred, and he sent orders for Drum to arrest Sitting Bull. Drum and McLaughlin decided to wait until Sitting Bull came to the agency to collect his rations and then have the Indian police arrest him. But when Sitting Bull expressed a desire to visit dancers on another reservation, McLaughlin felt compelled to act.

Before dawn on December 15, 1890, Sitting Bull and his family were awakened by a pounding on the door of their log cabin. The Indian police stormed through the door, grabbed the chief, and

*The tragedy of Wounded Knee: dead Indians
lie in the snow after the massacre.*

shoved him outside. A crowd soon gathered, some
yelling at the police, some telling Sitting Bull to
resist, and others urging him to cooperate. In the
chaos of the moment, a shot rang out and hit Bull
Head, the commander of the Indian police. The
shooter was Catch-the-Bear, a longtime supporter
of Sitting Bull. As Bull Head fell to the ground, he
fired at Sitting Bull, hitting him in the chest.
Another officer shot the chief in the head. As the
meadowlark had foretold seven years earlier,
Sitting Bull had been killed by his own people.

In the next few minutes, six of Sitting Bull's
supporters, including Catch-the-Bear, Jumping
Bull, and his son, were killed, as were six police-
men. When the police entered Sitting Bull's cabin,
they found 14-year-old Crow Foot hiding under a
blanket and shot him.

The tragedy at Standing Rock was followed two weeks later by a tragedy on a much larger scale. The army had been ordered to arrest Big Foot, a Miniconjou chief who had fought alongside Sitting Bull in the struggle against the wasichus. Big Foot's band had heard about the death of Sitting Bull, and they feared a similar fate for themselves. They were making their way toward Pine Ridge when they were intercepted by the cavalry and ordered to go to a camp on Wounded Knee Creek.

The Indians went along peacefully, and when they reached Wounded Knee the soldiers began to confiscate their weapons. A shot rang out, no one knew if it came from a soldier's gun or the gun of an Indian, and bedlam broke loose. The soldiers shot into the crowd, and before they finished, at least 200 Lakota were dead. The Wounded Knee Massacre killed any hope that the Ghost Dance religion might have restored in the Sioux.

At the Chicago World's Fair in 1892, crowds gathered to see Sitting Bull's cabin, which had been transported from Standing Rock for the occasion. Even after death, Sitting Bull was marketed as the man who killed Custer. But over a century later, Sitting Bull is remembered as a defender of freedom and a man of great strength and integrity who led his people through the most difficult time in their history.

CHRONOLOGY

1834?   Sitting Bull is born.

1851   Indian tribes and the U.S. government sign the Treaty of Fort Laramie.

1854   The Gratten Massacre causes the U.S. government to send more soldiers to the Great Plains.

1857   Sitting Bull is named war chief of the Hunkpapa.

1862   Gold is discovered in the Rocky Mountains, leading to a rush of settlers. The Dakota people, after not receiving promised annuities, attack and murder several settlers. The Dakotas are defeated by the U.S. Army, who press on into Lakota territory, causing war.

1863   Sitting Bull fights the U.S. cavalry. The
        Battle of Killdeer Mountain ends with
        more than 100 Indians killed and the
        Lakota flee. Sitting Bull is wounded in
        the hip.

1865   Some Lakota gather at Fort Sully to
        sign treaties with the U.S. government.
        Sitting Bull refuses to participate.

1866   Eighty-one U.S. soldiers are killed by
        Oglala Sioux at the Fetterman
        Massacre.

1867   Sitting Bull holds Fort Buford in a state
        of siege.

1868   A new Fort Laramie Treaty is signed,
        but Sitting Bull again refuses to trust
        the whites.

1869   Sitting Bull becomes the chief of the
        entire Sioux nation.

1874   General Custer leads an armed expedi-
        tion into the Black Hills, breaking the
        Fort Laramie Treaty of 1868. The U.S.
        government begins by trying to buy the
        land from the Indians. When the Indians

refuse, the government resolves to use force.

1876   Custer and his men are wiped out by Sitting Bull's Sioux forces at the Battle of Little Bighorn.

1877   Sitting Bull and his remaining followers flee the United States and enter Canada.

1881   Sitting Bull surrenders at Fort Buford.

1883   As part of a delegation of Sioux, Sitting Bull travels to Bismarck, North Dakota.

1885   Sitting Bull joins Buffalo Bill's Wild West Show and tours all over the United States.

1889   The Ghost Dance religion sweeps through the Sioux Indian reservations.

1890   Sitting Bull is shot and killed when Indian agents come to arrest him.

GLOSSARY

agency administrative centers on reservations, where government agents gave the Indians annuities

annuities food and goods provided to the Indians from the U.S. government as part of a treaty

band a group of families that lived together; several bands made up a tribe

butte an isolated hill or mountain

confiscate to seize and take over

coup stick a weapon used in hand-to-hand fighting to knock out the opponent

Great Plains the dry, mostly flat area of land between the Mississippi River and the Rocky Mountains

Jesuit a religious order called the Roman Catholic Society of Jesus

missionary a person who travels to a foreign land to spread the teachings of Christianity

raid a small, quick attack that is designed to take the enemy by surprise

reservation land set aside by the government for American Indians

Sun Dance a ceremony where Lakota men endured personal sacrifice to the Wakantanka

surveyor a person who maps and charts a piece of land

vision quest the important spiritual meeting of a young boy and his guardian spirit

Wakantanka the name given by the Lakota to the sacred power present throughout the universe

wasichu a Lakota word meaning "white people"

way station a stopping place on a journey to another location

A NOTE ON SOURCES

An excellent comprehensive biography of Sitting Bull is Robert M. Utley's *The Lance and the Shield: The Life and Times of Sitting Bull* (New York: Henry Holt, 1993). It provides detailed and accurate information on the chief's life. The insight it offers into Sitting Bull's personal life and the motivations for his actions puts a human face on a man who has been built into a larger-than-life character. Utley also does a terrific job explaining the historical forces that were at work at the time. Alexander B. Adams's *Sitting Bull: An Epic of the Plains* (New York: Putnam, 1973) gives further explanation of the political motivation behind the U.S. government's treatment of the Sioux. Adams tells the story of the Sioux wars from both sides of the conflict, alternating between the experiences and perceptions of the Sioux and those of the U.S. soldiers, politicians, and citizens.

Although Stanley Vestal's *Sitting Bull: Champion of the Sioux* (Norman and London: University of Oklahoma Press, 1932) is written in a dated, often dramatic style intended to glorify the accomplishments of Sitting Bull, it provides some interesting details of his life through the first-hand accounts of Sitting Bull's nephews and others who knew him.

Dee Brown's *Bury My Heart at Wounded Knee* (New York: Henry Holt, 1970) puts the struggles of the Lakota into the context of what was happening throughout the West. It contains accounts of many of the battles fought between the United States and the western American Indian tribes in the second half of the 19th century.

For insight into the spirituality that was central to Sitting Bull's life, I turned to John G. Neihardt's *Black Elk Speaks: Being the Life Story of a Holy Man of the Oglala Sioux* (Lincoln and London: University of Nebraska Press, 1932). Based on interviews with a holy man who grew up during the Sioux wars, it offers personal insights into traditional religious experiences, such as the vision quest and the Sun Dance, as well as the Ghost Dance religion, and it offers first-hand accounts of the Oglala's interactions with whites.

FOR MORE INFORMATION

BOOKS

Bachrach, Deborah. *Custer's Last Stand: Opposing Viewpoints*. San Diego: Greenhaven Press, 1990.

Bonvillain, Nancy. *Teton Sioux*. New York: Chelsea House, 1994.

Brown, Dee. *Wounded Knee: An Indian History of the American West*. New York: Henry Holt, 1974.

Dunn, John M. *The Relocation of the North American Indian*. San Diego: Lucent Books, 1995.

St. George, Judith. *Crazy Horse*. New York: Putnam, 1994.

INTERNET SITES

Because of the changeable nature of the Internet, sites appear and disappear very quickly. These resources offered useful information on the Lakota Sioux at the time of publication. Internet addresses must be entered with capital and lowercase letters exactly as they appear.

http://www.lakhota.com/default.htm
This is the homepage for Sioux Heritage. There are links to cultural pages, references and resources, and a language program.

http://www.lakhota.com/sdnation.htm
This site is maintained by the South Dakota Tourist Bureau and provides a list of sites and locations of Lakota culture and history in South Dakota.

INDEX

ABOUT THE AUTHOR

Catherine Iannone studied cultural anthropology at Wesleyan University and has edited a number of books on Native American tribes and notable Native Americans. She is also the author of *Pocahontas, the Powhatan Princess* (Chelsea House Publishers).